W9-BCR-402

Liberation

Teens in the Concentration Camps and
the Teen Soldiers Who Liberated Them

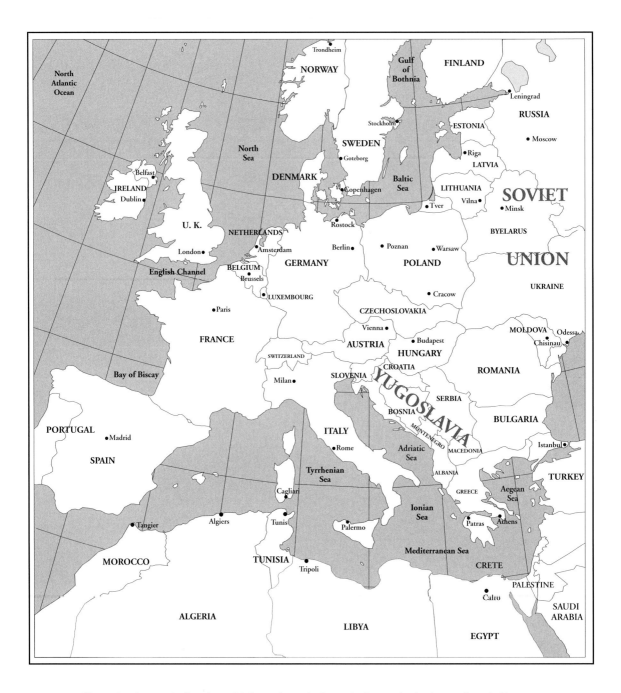

The Nazis and their allies invaded and devastated most of Europe
and North Africa.

Liberation

Teens in the Concentration Camps and the Teen Soldiers Who Liberated Them

E. Tina Tito

THE ROSEN PUBLISHING GROUP, INC.
NEW YORK

*I would like to thank Dina Dadush and Ilan and Gabrielle Tito for their
assistance with this book.*

Published in 1999 by The Rosen Publishing Group, Inc.
29 East 21st Street, New York, NY 10010

First Edition

Library of Congress Cataloging-in-Publication Data

Tito, E. Tina, 1948–
    Liberation : teens in the concentration camps and the teen soldiers
who liberated them / E. Tina Tito.
        p.   cm. — (Teen witnesses to the Holocaust)
    Includes bibliographical references and index.
    Summary: Tells the story, in their own words, of two survivors of
World War II concentration camps, and two American soldiers
who helped liberate the camps.
        ISBN 0-8239-2846-2
    1. Holocaust, Jewish (1939–1945)—Juvenile literature. 2. Jewish
children in the Holocaust—Juvenile literature. 3. World War,
1939–1945—Concentration camps—Liberation—Juvenile literature.
[1. Holocaust, Jewish (1939–1945)—Personal narratives. 2. Jews—
Biography. 3. World War, 1939–1945—Concentration camps.] I. Title.
II. Series.
D804.34.T57 1998
940.53'18'0835—dc21
                                                                98-33497
                                                                    CIP
                                                                     AC

Manufactured in the United States of America

Contents

Introduction

It is important for everyone to learn about the Holocaust, the systematic murder of 6 million Jews during World War II (1939–1945). It is a dark scar across the face of human history. As a student, you are part of the future generation that will lead and guide the family of humankind. Your proper understanding of the Holocaust is essential. You will learn its lessons. You will be able to ensure that a Holocaust will never happen again and that the world will be a safe place for each person—regardless of his or her nationality, religion, or ethnicity.

Nazi Germany added a dangerous new element to the familiar concept of "dislike of the unlike." The Nazis introduced the idea that an *ethnic group* whom someone dislikes or hates can be isolated from the rest of the population and earmarked for total destruction, *without any possibility of survival.*

The Nazis chose the Jewish people for this fatal annihilation. Their definition of a Jew was a uniquely racial one: a person with Jewish blood. To the Nazis, a person with even one Jewish grandparent was a Jew—a person to be killed.

The Germans systematically rounded up Jews in the countries that they occupied during World War II. They built death camps equipped with the most sophisticated technology available in order to kill the Jews. With the assistance of collaborators (non-Germans who willingly helped), they murdered more than 6 million Jews. Among the victims were 1.5 million children and teenagers. These Jewish children, like

American troops bound for the war in Europe wave good-bye to family and friends.

Jewish adults, had no options. They were murdered because they had Jewish blood, and nothing they could do could change that.

Such a thing had never happened before in recorded history, despite the fact that genocide (deliberate destruction of people of one ethnic, political, or cultural group) had occurred. In the past, victims or oppressed people were usually offered an option to avoid death: they could change their religion, or be expelled to another country. But the Nazi concept of racism did not give the victim any possibility for survival, since a person cannot change his or her blood, skin color, or eye color.

A few non-Jewish people, known as the Righteous Among the Nations, saved Jews from death. They felt that they were their brothers' and sisters' keepers. But they were in the minority. The majority were collaborators or bystanders. During the Holocaust, I was a young child saved by several Righteous Poles. The majority of my family and the Jews of my town, many of whose families had lived there for 900 years, were murdered by the Nazis with the assistance of local collaborators. Photographs of those who were murdered gaze upon visitors to the Tower of Life exhibit that I designed for the United States Holocaust Memorial Museum in Washington, D.C.

We must learn the lessons of the Holocaust. We must learn to respect one another, regardless of differences in religion, ethnicity, or race, since we all belong to the family of humankind. The United States and Canada are both countries of immigrants, populated by many ethnic groups. In lands of such diversity, dislike of the unlike—the Nazi idea of using racial classification as a reason to destroy other humans—is dangerous to all of us. If we allow intolerance toward one group of people today, any of us could be part of a group selected for destruction tomorrow. Understanding and respecting one another regardless of religion, race, or ethnicity, is essential for coexistence and survival.

In this book individuals who were teenagers during the Holocaust share their experiences of life before and during the war and of the days of liberation. Their messages about their families, friends, love, suffering, survival, liberation, and rebuilding of new lives are deeply inspiring. They are important because these survivors are among the last eyewitnesses, the last links to what happened during the Holocaust.

I hope that their stories will encourage you to build a better, safer future "with liberty and justice for all."

Yaffa Eliach, Ph.D.
Professor of History and Literature
Department of Judaic Studies, Brooklyn College

chapter one

A Shocking Discovery

During the summer of 1944, as World War II raged on, American forces landed in Normandy, France, to fight against Nazi Germany. Most soldiers left the United States prepared to give their lives to keep Adolf Hitler and his allies from conquering all of Europe. They brought with them their youth, their training, and their American viewpoint. However imperfectly carried out in the United States, the American ideals of democracy and equality were nonetheless ones that most soldiers had been taught to respect.

American troops had been trained to battle German troops on land and sea and in the air. They had only vaguely heard about Nazi concentration camps from the Army newspaper, *Stars and Stripes*. Those American soldiers who came upon the concentration camps did not know what they were. They did not at first understand why the camps had been set up: to kill those the Nazis deemed unworthy of life—either by slave labor and deprivation, or by gassing.

Of the 6 million European Jews killed by the Nazis, most were murdered in the camps. The soldiers who liberated the camps had not been prepared by their commanding officers to witness the tragic human cost of Nazi "racial" theory.

Survivors of Dachau concentration camp cheer the arrival of American soldiers, who liberated the camp on April 29, 1945.

Hitler's Destructive Vision

Eleven years earlier, in 1933, Adolf Hitler and his National Socialist (Nazi) Party had come to power in Germany. At that time, Germany was experiencing the Depression: unemployment was widespread, and spirits were low. The Nazis promised to make Germany great again.

Hitler blamed Germany's problems on the Jews. Hitler claimed that the Germanic peoples, the Aryans, were the only race capable of building a great civilization. But he said the "inferior" populations of Europe, and particularly the Jews, had polluted the "pure" blood of the Aryans. Nazi theory said that the Aryan "master race" needed more living space to develop to its full potential. To the Nazis, it made sense to enslave—or eliminate—"inferior" peoples and seize their land.

In the early 1930s, once the Nazis were in power, all political, religious, and intellectual leaders in Germany who opposed Hitler's policies were persecuted and placed in concentration camps. These camps were places of cruelty: prisoners were subjected to forced labor, beatings, torture, humiliation, and starvation. At the same time, the rights of German Jews were gradually being taken away.

In September 1939 Germany went to war. Over time, the Jews in Germany and all the Nazi-occupied countries of Europe were isolated from mainstream society and placed in ghettos: enclosed, guarded slum quarters in large cities. Beginning in 1941, many Jews in the former Soviet Union were executed, usually by the *Einsatzgruppen*—mobile killing squads that followed the German army and killed Jews and sometimes Russians in the newly occupied territories. The Germans were often helped in their efforts by local populations. In 1942, the Nazis implemented the "Final Solution," a plan to murder the Jews, most of whom were now trapped in ghettos or camps. Jewish men, women, and children were sent to camps to die a slow death or be killed outright.

The Allies Approach

When the American troops landed, the Germans were losing the war. As American troops advanced, guards at Nazi concentration camps

Former inmates of the concentration camp at Ebensee, Austria, leave
the camp after being liberated by the U.S. Third Army.
Overhead a sign reads, "We welcome our liberators."

were ordered to take camp inmates on death marches deep into
Germany, away from the Allied troops. Nazi wardens were given
orders to kill any prisoner who slowed down the death marches.
They were also ordered to destroy any traces of incriminating
evidence before the Allied troops discovered the labor camps,
concentration camps, and death camps the Nazis invented to kill the
Jews of Europe, their so-called enemies.

Meanwhile, many camp inmates realized from the approaching
gunfire that liberation was possible. They sought hiding places.
Prisoners did not appear at the required morning attendance-taking,
the *Zeilappell*. Tower guards, too, were not necessarily at their posts.

By spring 1945 American GIs had liberated eleven camps:
Buchenwald, Dachau, Dora-Mittelbau, Flossenbürg, Ebensee,
Gunskirchen, Güsen, Landsberg, Mauthausen, Ohrdruf, and

General Dwight Eisenhower and other U.S. Army officers view the bodies of executed prisoners at the concentration camp in Ohrdruf, Germany.

Wöbbelin. The soldiers sometimes came upon raggedly clad skeletons wandering along the roads, abandoned by Nazi guards as the gunfire of American troops neared.

Into the Camps

As American soldiers passed through the gates and barbed-wire fences of the camps, they were completely shocked. While prepared for war, they were unprepared for genocide. They saw stacks of dead bodies and the wasted figures of inmates. The soldiers were overcome by the terrible odors everywhere.

The survivors who could muster enough energy to show their joy and excitement fell to their knees and kissed the boots of the soldiers, crying with happiness. The sick and weak showed their feelings through tear-rimmed eyes. The young soldiers understood how welcome they were. Many of the inmates could not believe that these uniformed soldiers had arrived to free them. Some survivors remained fearful, believing that the Nazi guards would come out at any moment and shoot them. They needed time to adjust to the fact that they had been liberated.

The survivors came from all the countries that had been occupied by the Nazis. Most were Jewish. Other camp survivors included Roma and Sinti (Gypsies), homosexuals, Jehovah's Witnesses, religious leaders from every religious group in Europe, political prisoners, and prisoners of war (POWS), including thousands of Russian and some American soldiers.

Generals Eisenhower, Bradley, and Patton came to the camps so that they could become eyewitnesses to the gas chambers, crematoria, and burial pits where millions of human beings had been murdered. Full military reports were made of the shocking evidence left behind by the Nazi perpetrators. The crematoria still had the smoldering remains of bodies in them. The sealed gas chambers had not all been torn down by the fleeing Germans, despite their efforts to hide what they had done.

Suddenly liberated, survivors wanted to know if any members of their families were alive. They were overwhelmed and fearful about their future. Who were they without their families? Where could they go? Did they have the strength to start their lives over?

Background photo: A stack of human corpses outside a crematorium at Buchenwald.

chapter two

Irving Roth

Irving Roth was born in Kosice, Czechoslovakia. His father, Joseph, was a successful businessman, and his mother, Helen, ran the household. Andre, his brother, was three years older.

In 1935, Irving's family moved to Humene, Slovakia, where they stayed until anti-Jewish laws made them hand over their business and homes to the Nazis. His family then moved to Budapest, Hungary, in the spring of 1943.

Irving, his parents, brother, grandfather, aunts, uncles, and cousins were rounded up with all the Jews of the area and ordered into the Budapest ghetto in spring 1944. In a few weeks, the Jewish residents of the ghetto were loaded onto trains and sent to the Auschwitz-Birkenau concentration camp in Poland. Irving's ailing father, who was in a hospital, and his mother were hidden by a Hungarian nurse and her family. All other family members were taken on the transport. It was May 1944.

Irving and his brother passed the initial selection at Auschwitz. The rest of the family were taken to the gas chambers upon arrival.

At Auschwitz, I was assigned to the fields from early morning until late at night, draining swamps and plowing the fields. As 1945 approached, everybody realized that the Russian army was getting closer and closer. There was this feeling that the Nazis might decide to simply liquidate the whole camp and shoot us all.

Suddenly January 18, 1945, came along. That's the day that my brother and I and about 60,000 other prisoners were marched out of Auschwitz toward Germany. It was a death march. The weather was freezing cold, and we walked a couple of days until we finally arrived at a place called Gleiwitz. We were loaded into open cattle cars and during the next day, two, or three we were shuttled back and forth, without any food or water, until we arrived at Buchenwald concentration camp, in Germany.

They called out the names of the youngest people. I, being one of the youngest (fifteen), was taken away to the Kleinelager, *the children's camp. I do not know exactly what happened to my brother. We did say good-bye to each other, saying we would meet up again soon, we hoped, because the war couldn't go on forever. Of course, our temporary separation was forever.

The Allies Advance

By 1945, I was down to about seventy-five pounds. I was fortunate that I did not have dysentery. I did have lice.

Emotionally, I suppose, we knew that the war was coming to an end, and the question was, "Am I going to survive?" The rate of death was tremendous because of disease and dysentery. There wasn't any sanitation or medicine—nothing. The objective was to try and stay alive.

A survivor of Buchenwald concentration camp. In the camps inmates were starved and worked to death.

15

We weren't sure of what was happening because of the constant rumors. One of the stories circulating was that, even if the American army did come, they might blow the place up.

At the end of March 1945, the Nazis started marching people out—another death march. By this time, many people realized that the idea was to stay in the camp. The chances of survival on a death march were very, very limited, particularly toward the end of the war, when there was a tremendous amount of killing going on.

Background photo: Inmates on a death march near Grünwald, Germany, April 1945.

You would think that the guards would have recognized that the war was coming to an end, that they would have said, "Hey, let me get out of here and save my own skin . . ." Unfortunately, the indoctrination was so powerful, and the hatred against the Jews so immense, that even at the last moments, people were shot.

As the evacuations started all over again, my goal was not to be taken. As they started selecting people for death marches, two inmates and I managed to hide. At one point we hid in the sewers, in the toilets, and under the buildings. I could crawl under the buildings; I was a skinny little kid.

On the tenth of April, you could no longer hide. The Nazi guards came in with dogs to ferret everybody out. There were about 10,000 people, maybe 8,000. I was among them, standing at the Appelplatz in front of the open gates of the camp. I knew very well that the death march would begin.

Then a miracle took place.

The alarm system went off because there was an air raid. As the alarm sounded, most of the guards—actually all the guards except for one—disappeared into the bunkers and hid, closing the gates as we stood there. Only one guard stayed for a while, and this guard pulled out his gun and started shooting at airplanes. The airplanes, of course, were at 10,000 feet, but he was Superman. It struck me as funny. Then he too left. We went back to our block and survived another day.

A Final Battle

The next day, the eleventh of April, at eleven AM, we were in the Kleinelager, close to the fence. Outside the electrified fence were the towers where the Nazi guards sat with submachine guns.

The guards suddenly disappeared. The young Polish Blockälteste really tried to calm us. He told us to lie down on the floor because there was going to be some shooting. We all lay down as flat as we could, ten of us, from about eleven AM to three PM, until the shooting died down.

Then the first two GIs I ever saw walked into the Kleinelager. One was black and one was white. As they walked into our block—I remember this clearly as day—they looked around at our emaciated young bodies. They had tears in their eyes and emptied their pockets of K-rations and cigarettes. That was liberation!

The soldiers brought water tanks and fed us. They gave us whatever was available in the camp: food from the pantries of the German soldiers and Nazi guards, mostly pork and dairy products that did not do our systems much good. Dysentery was prevalent. Most of us were in pretty rotten shape. Fortunately, the medics came in right after them, and they realized that you can't start giving emaciated kids milk and meat. They needed to be

Accompanied by American soldiers, young survivors of Buchenwald
walk out through the main gates of the camp.

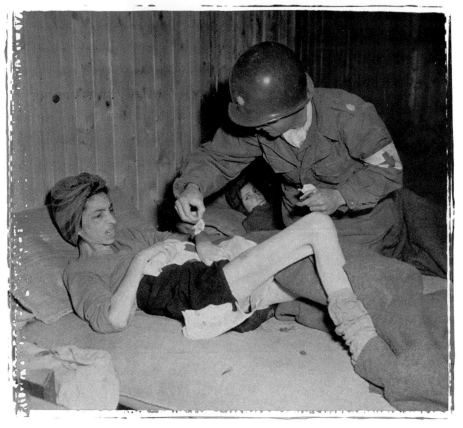

Lt. Col. J. W. Branch, chief surgeon of the Sixth Armored Division, Third Army, dresses sores on a Hungarian survivor in Penig, Germany, a sub-camp of Buchenwald, April 26, 1945.

much more careful, so rice and cereal were brought in on the second and third days.

Since my friends and I were kids, we were resilient, and I think most of us who had made it to that moment survived. Seeing the Nazi guards disappear, seeing the Americans come in, seeing the gates opened, seeing the barbed wire "disappear," so to speak—there wasn't any question in my mind that I was still alive. This nightmare was over. During the first day there were moments of euphoria.

Before liberation, my death sentence was apparent. I had gone through the whole business of selection in Auschwitz more than once, the process of marching on a death march—people being shot right and left for no particular reason. All this was suddenly lifted. There was a sudden transformation. It's like decompression—a sudden decompression, immediate.

There was, however, the next day.

Finding a Way Home

As this whole thing settled in my mind, the questions kept coming: Where was everybody? What had happened? Was I the only one from the whole family alive?

The first thing I did, the second or third day, was start walking up and down the camp looking for a familiar face. I saw a small entourage, maybe three, four people, walking with someone. He was wearing an American uniform. I looked at him, and he told us in Yiddish that he was a rabbi from America. I remembered one of my American relatives who was a rabbi in Brooklyn. His name was Wallberg, and this man sort of looked like him.

Hey, with my luck, I thought, maybe this was Rabbi Wallberg, and that would be a miracle! It turned out that it was not him.

I did not ask him if he knew my mother's cousin Wallberg in New York. That was a mistake. This gentleman was Rabbi Herschel Schechter, and I spoke to him many years later here in America. I told him the story and he said, "Why didn't you tell me? I knew your cousin very well. We were both teachers on the faculty of Yeshiva University in New York."

Nevertheless, I kind of followed him around. We went into one of the buildings, where I found two people from my town. Suddenly, I wasn't totally alone. We talked for a while, and we all decided to go back together to Czechoslovakia at the end of the war.

As we were planning our future, we shed the striped uniforms. The GIs opened up the commissary, the clothing operation of the Nazi army. I now possessed a pair of new boots and a total uniform that was normally for Nazi soldiers. We took all the Nazi markings off, and the American soldiers gave us little gray five-pointed stars that we proudly put on. We stayed in Buchenwald and got fed and deloused and everything else that was necessary.

One of the things that everybody got was a carton of cigarettes, Camels. I didn't smoke. Being fifteen years old and trying to belong, I opened a pack of cigarettes and lit up. I didn't inhale because I didn't have the foggiest notion how to smoke. That night, as I went to sleep, my tongue burned. I thought this was insanity. Why would anyone subject themselves to pain after all we had gone through? I

traded my cigarettes with the smokers for their chocolates, K-rations—
wonderful stuff. I find that I am a chocoholic to this day.

The Army moved us, the young people, into some of the Nazi
headquarters. We were treated well by the Americans.

We were able to go into the nearby town, Weimar. I think it is
ironic: Weimar and Buchenwald. Weimar represented the first
experiment in German democracy. Buchenwald was an experiment
in the most vile oppression.

American Outrage

I think that by April 1945 the medics knew how to handle the
situation because they had been through a few other places. The
combat troops were prepared for finding people in POW camps, but
they knew nothing about the extent of the deprivation in the camps
created by the Nazi system. They learned very quickly.

One Sunday afternoon, a week or two later, the American
commander decided to bring German townspeople in from Weimar to
see what had taken place and to help bury the dead. These people
looked somewhat somber, but it was obvious that they knew who we
were because we were only about seven or ten miles from Weimar.
Many of the prisoners, preceding liberation, had been taken through
Weimar to defuse Allied bombs that did not explode. Who do you use
for defusing bombs? Prisoners—so if and when the bombs went off, it
would only kill a bunch of people who were to be killed anyway.

Buchenwald was set up as a concentration camp, not a death camp.
There were no gas chambers, just crematoria. Burnt bodies were still
found in the oven area after liberation. The American soldiers brought
people in from the towns because of their own sense of outrage at what
they had witnessed at the camp.

At the end of the war, May 1945, the American army took us by truck
to Pilsen, in Czechoslovakia. Soon after, I met someone who told me that
my parents were still alive. I went to where they were living.

It was a bittersweet reunion: my brother was not with us.

German civilians are brought to the Wöbbelin concentration camp to
view the corpses of prisoners.

chapter three

Jim Van Raalte

Jim Van Raalte was born in New York City. His father worked at the Van Raalte Company, founded by Jim's grandfather. It made hosiery, lingerie, and gloves for women. Jim's mother was a homemaker. After high school, Jim went into the production and sales end of the family business. He attended Brown University with his twin brother, Tom.

When the U.S. draft laws of 1940 were established, Tom and Jim knew that they would be drafted. They enlisted in the Army in December 1942 and trained with the Signal Corps. They went into officer's training for three months. Jim flunked out but was made a noncommissioned sergeant. His brother was sent to North Africa.

I was sent to England with the 3103rd Signal Battalion. In the fall of 1943 we came over, sleeping on hammocks suspended near the boiler room on a British passenger ship called the Mauritania.

We got off the ship in the middle of the night, and we were put up in private homes in Dudley. In the morning, the villagers did not know what to make of us. We were not allowed to talk to anyone. Unknown to us, FBI agents intermingled in our outfit to make sure everything was going exactly as planned—no spies or men doing their job improperly.

Our battalion was about to take on a very secretive operation. The primary thing that we did from fall 1943 until spring 1944 was to send false signals, before D-Day, across the English Channel to the Germans. We simulated a whole battalion training opposite the Germans who, we knew, were stationed in Calais, France. It turns out that we decoyed whole Panzer divisions away from Normandy, the actual place planned for the landing of the Allied invasion forces. Because of our operation, the Germans thought we were going to hit them right in Calais.

I was in Company C, and our men came from all walks of life— butchers, farmers, accountants—and from all religions and colors. We were trained as radio operators or repairmen. There weren't many blacks in our company but I remember, as a noncom sergeant, I had my own squad room. I slept next to three black soldiers. They were wonderful guys.

I remember a United Service Organizations (USO) dance in Dudley where we had a very bad experience. Somehow a riot broke out between the blacks and other members of our battalion. Fighting broke out, and men were cut up. I and my men had to block anyone from coming into Dudley. It was ugly. Later, there was a big lineup of the whole battalion in the streets of Dudley. FBI agents went through and asked us questions, and then the whole thing seemed to blow over.

In June 1944, we were sent over to France by our commanding officer, Captain Deutch, to prepare for the Normandy Invasion, D-Day. We were attached to the 10th Photo Reconnaissance Group. These guys went up in planes and took photographs of any German installation they thought important. The planes were not armed, but they were accompanied by a fighter plane.

Our group served as communications on the ground for these planes. The name of our installation was Gander. It was harrowing waiting for them to come back. If the returning plane shot flares into the sky, we knew that there were wounded on board. There were times the planes did not come back. Their crew chiefs on the ground were heartbroken.

June 6, 1944, was D-Day. The sky turned black with our planes going over to liberate France.

The Normandy Invasion lasted until August 1944.

Battle of the Bulge

One night, around December 1944, we were holed up in a barn. Suddenly we were being shot at, and the bullets were landing and marking the edges of my sleeping bag. We got out of there and had a layover in Verdun, in eastern France, until we got notice that the Battle of the Bulge was breaking out.

My men and I were attached to the 87th Acorn Infantry Division, in a very small town close to Verdun. We were taken into the woods and had 87th Division patches sewn on our uniforms. We camouflaged the trucks with 87th Division infantry insignias and walked around the town acting as decoys so that the German soldiers hidden there would think that the 87th was in the vicinity. It got dicey. We made it through, but it was chaos. During the shooting that broke out it was hard to tell who was an ally and who was an enemy.

My men and I had little field sets for communication. One man was the operator, and the other man ran the generator for power, grinding and pumping out the supply of energy, as one would pedal a bicycle. It was exhausting. We were fired at and dumped on, but somehow we always made it out. We had a grenade on our radio set so that we could blow it up immediately in case we were overrun by German soldiers. Fortunately, this never happened to us, although I witnessed a lot of death around me. We got very close to the men we were with under these circumstances. There was no such thing as discrimination. We were buddies, and we were going to look out for each other. We always talked about getting out of the Army. We practiced how we would talk on the boat heading home, trying to say one sentence without a swear word. The war was hard on us.

Ghostly, Ghastly

After the Bulge, we were attached to Patton's Third Army, 80th Infantry. We had established fixed communications stations, which were huge two-ton trucks with canvas on them. It was quite sophisticated compared to the field sets. We sat inside the trucks, under the canvas.

American soldiers view human corpses outside the crematorium at Buchenwald.

We got word that there was something pretty bad up ahead. It happened to be Buchenwald. The infantrymen were coming out of there stunned and couldn't talk about it. My company commander said that I was to bring in the truck with my seven men. He said that some noncoms there would show me where to establish the radio stations and lay the wiring. On the road into Buchenwald, we saw no one. We drove in very slowly.

It was like another world. We couldn't believe what we were seeing. It was quiet, so quiet. Here and there we could see a prisoner walking around. They could hardly walk. They were skin and bones, dark eyes, sallow complexions.

We stopped the truck. A small group of prisoners gathered behind the truck and called out, "Cigarettes, cigarettes." One guy came up to get a cigarette and lit it. All of a sudden, he ran back to this prisoner who had one leg and was leaning on a cane. He gave the cigarette to him. His compassion struck me at the time, and I still haven't forgotten the incident. We gave out all the cigarettes that we had.

Our company commander instructed us to place guards around the truck and set up radio contact. He told us we should take a look around. He thought we wouldn't have to report back right away. A Belgian prisoner came up to us and offered to take us around. He wasn't in bad shape, and he spoke a little English.

The first thing he showed us was a row of twenty six-foot stakes, planted side by side. He stated that the prisoners had been stripped, chained to the posts, drenched with water, beaten, and forced to remain on the posts for days. Other prisoners were brought to view them until they died. Then they were placed, dead, in a yard, about the size of a city block, one on top of the other.

They were not really piled, but dumped as a little girl might discard a rag doll. The pile was now about twenty-five feet square and hip high. These were the remnants of the bodies that the Germans didn't have time to shove into the furnaces before they took off.

Terror was written all over the faces of the dead corpses. Their mouths were wide-open, gaping eyes staring out into space. There were bloody stumps in places where an arm or leg should have been. The

Corporal Larry Mutinsk distributes his last pack of cigarettes to the reaching hands of liberated prisoners at a camp in Allach, Germany.

place stank with all these dead bodies around. The Americans had to dump lye over everything, even the bodies. It was sheer horror. We couldn't believe it.

We moved on and saw that charred bodies were still in the four furnaces. They were burned from head to toe but one man hadn't disintegrated yet. The ashes from these burnings went through a trapdoor down to the lower floor, where they were collected to be used as fertilizer. It was such a methodical process. It was a business, a factory making finished goods. This "death" was well organized. That is what it was all about to the Nazis.

The barracks had three-tiered wooden bunks inside. The prisoners slept one on top of another. They were stashed in there like bolts of cloth in a textile mill.

We entered the barracks. One person was lying on his back with his head hanging over the foot of the bunk, and another person was lying on his stomach with his head hanging over. Men were sitting on the floor and, no matter where they were, they all took their hats off to us. It was awful. I felt like a Roman conqueror rather than a man who just wanted to help them out. I knew that they wanted to show how grateful they were. I was overwhelmed.

The U.S. Army was taking villagers who lived in the area through the camp. These people acted like they couldn't believe it. They were crying and saying, "Nein, nein, you know this didn't happen." That got me very angry because I was an impressionable kid, and they were a bunch of miserable people, pulling this kind of act after all that they had seen. There was certainly smoke from the many furnaces that had billowed into the skies around them for all those years.

When we finally drove out in our communications truck, the men were very still. One of my guys said, "Van, who the hell is going to believe this?" That is all we said to each other. It was overwhelming. It's as if we had seen space aliens walking around. That's the kind of world it was: eerie, ghostly, ghastly. We all wanted to get out.

When we got back to camp we started throwing things, cursing. We were real angry. We couldn't sleep for nights. No one had prepared us.

Former prisoners of the *Kleinelager* in Buchenwald stare out from the wooden barracks.

chapter four

Helen Tilles

Helen Tilles was born in Vienna, Austria. She had three older brothers, Nathan, Joseph, and Morris, and two half sisters. Her family moved to Cracow, Poland, when Helen was very young.

Helen's family owned a shoe store, where Helen's parents worked until her father's death. Helen's oldest brother, Nathan, ran the shop until 1934, when their mother, too, died.

Helen lived with Nathan, his wife, and their small children. She fulfilled her mother's wish that she be proficient in secretarial skills and study languages. Little did she know that these skills would save her life.

Helen had Jewish and non-Jewish friends and remembers playing around the beautiful grounds of the church on her street. Although she lost her parents at a young age, her family gave her a loving, happy life.

I couldn't believe that anything very bad was going to happen when the Germans marched into Poland in September 1939. During World War I my parents were not affected, as Jews, by the Germans, and my father had been a soldier for the Austrian army.

We all thought, at the beginning, that the problems would pass. We had to put on armbands signifying to all that we were Jews, and German soldiers came to our door and confiscated our radio. Eventually, my brother's beautiful apartment was handed over to

Jews wearing white armbands with blue stars are forced to shovel snow from the sidewalk in Cracow.

another family, and we had to find lodgings somewhere else. It got around that Cracow was to be Judenfrei *[free of Jews], so people moved out to small towns. Young people fled to the East. I was active in the Zionist movement and fled to Lvov, in eastern Poland, around 1940, when my boyfriend, Albert Tilles, decided to go there.*

In March 1941, the Germans established a Jewish ghetto in Cracow. All Jewish residents in and around Cracow were forced to leave their homes and move into the ghetto, including Helen's brothers.

Meanwhile, Lvov and the rest of eastern Poland had been invaded by the Russians. As a result, conditions in Lvov were becoming increasingly risky for Helen.

My boyfriend and I were not natives of Lvov, with no family or friends there. This was dangerous because the Russians were taking the foreigners for forced labor in Siberia. By 1942 my brother Nathan, by paying a lot of money, found two Polish men who agreed to give us false papers and bring us back to him in the Cracow ghetto.

Background photo: View of the gate of the Cracow ghetto.

33

Second Lieutenant Charlotte Chaney was a registered nurse in the U.S. Army during World War II. Although not a teenager at the time, she was part of an evacuation hospital that entered Dachau when it was liberated.

We came in as a hospital unit to take care and help with these people. That's why we took over all the German barracks where the German soldiers themselves stayed and cleaned them out and put the people in. We would take them from the compound where they were and put them into beds, clean beds, and clean them up and start them on medication and food and everything else. It was almost a twenty-four-hour continuous working around the clock.

The patients didn't know what was happening to them. And even when we fed them we had to start off gradually because there was malnutrition. We would start off with cereal and give them a little bread, and they would grab it and hide it under their pillows. When we would make the bed up we would find food hidden because they were afraid it would be taken away.

We tried to explain to them that they would get as much as they want now: whatever they wanted they will have, they didn't have to hide anything, or if they're hungry they would be given food. All these years that they had nothing—they just couldn't comprehend what was going on.

The Horror Increases

In 1942, the Germans began transporting the residents of the Cracow ghetto to concentration camps.

In spring 1942 we were all taken to Plaszow concentration camp. The old people and the young children—including my brothers' young children—were shot in Cracow as we were loaded onto the trains.

In Plaszow, I worked in a tailor shop. The food was horrible, but since we were working they gave us larger rations. We wore dresses with white stripes painted on them. I eventually got work as a typist because I had secretarial training. They also took me because I spoke German fluently.

It was warm in the camp administration building, and people treated us properly. There were periodic transports out of the camp. Many men—including my three brothers—were taken in September 1944. Soon after, they took my two nieces and girlfriends on a transport. I stayed with 500 other young, healthy girls who had the skills the Germans needed at Plaszow.

On January 14, 1945, the Germans screamed, "Out! Take what you have with you!" The only things we had were a blanket, a soup dish, and a spoon. We were wearing light coats and a blanket, but I was lucky: I still had my leather boots.

We were marched through Cracow. The Polish people looked at the Jews without blinking an eye, never saying or handing out anything.

I marched for four days, and at night I slept on hay in barns. I was freezing. The guards were German and Ukrainian. It was possible to escape, but where would I get shelter? Who would help me? I decided to stay.

We finally arrived in Auschwitz, Poland. We were evacuated, with everyone else, the very next day. We began to hear the sounds of war planes. I found two of my nieces in Auschwitz, and we marched out together. We marched for two days, and then we were put on trains.

We arrived at Bergen-Belsen concentration camp in Germany. I was searched upon arrival by other female inmates. One of these girls took my boots off my feet and handed me wooden clogs. Now everything became more difficult.

Bergen-Belsen was a horrible place. No food at all. We saw a lot of dead bodies. Women were lying all over the place, in trenches, all dying of starvation and typhus. We were full of lice. We were given soup once a day, no bread.

Someone was looking for young, strong girls to work in a munitions factory in southern Germany. I volunteered myself, two friends, and my two nieces. A few hundred girls left that day. The only thing one could do at Bergen-Belsen was die. We had to get out. I think I lost my belief in God in Bergen-Belsen after the horrors I saw there.

Human corpses, discovered in a mass grave at Bergen-Belsen, just before they were buried by Canadian and British liberators.

A crematorium oven in Bergen-Belsen after liberation, 1945.

Evacuated and Turned Away

It was February 1945. We went on trains to the labor camp in Venusberg, Germany. Some food was given to us there, and we went to work. They asked if someone spoke German. I stepped forward, and I was lucky again. I worked in the office, registering the people and giving out food ration cards. There were a lot of air raids. We prayed that they would hit this underground munitions camp and stop our misery. The planes never came near us.

People were coming down with typhus. I finally contracted typhus and was placed in one of the makeshift hospitals for a few days. It was around April 1945. The Germans came in and said, "Out!" They were evacuating the camp. Sick or not, you had to go. We marched and marched. I could hardly move, and they shot you if you slowed down. Almost all of us were suffering from different stages of typhus. We finally arrived at the train station, and we were placed in open cattle cars: no food, no shelter, and it was still cold.

As we arrived at different camps, no one would take us in. Every camp was evacuating. We started to have a lot of deaths, and we had to throw the bodies, hundreds of them, off the train. They were mainly Hungarian. These beautiful young girls were new to this life, since the Nazis had come into Hungary late in 1944. I was hardened by all I had been through already. Half of us—250 women—died in this transport.

As the train passed through Czechoslovakia, people stood with kettles of soup and loaves of bread, handing them out to us over the sides of the open train cars as our train stopped at the stations. They cried bitter tears for us. These were the only times we were fed.

The trip took sixteen days and nights. We arrived at Mauthausen concentration camp, a men's camp in Austria, in early May 1945. They let us unload ourselves in front of the crematoria. We didn't even know where we were. The crematoria were so overloaded with bodies that they had to put us in the men's barracks.

Liberation

On May 5, we woke up on the floor, listening to strange sounds. We looked at the watchtowers. There were no Germans, no guards. We saw stacks and stacks of dead male bodies outside. We all left the barracks. We knew something was happening.

We saw a tank and an American soldier. He started screaming, "You are free! Come out!" The strangest thing happened. There was no jubilation. A sound of horrible moaning started. Everybody was crying. They started thinking of those that did not make it to this moment.

More tanks came. More soldiers. I think it was a unit of the Eighth Army. The most wonderful people in the world. It was an American military field hospital. They started organizing immediately, passing out medications. There were nurses, doctors. The soldiers started feeding us. Excellent food, rich and fat. Our stomachs could not tolerate the fat. People started getting very sick. I was one of the luckier ones. I was so sick from typhus that I could not swallow anything. That was my luck. At least 3,000 people died at Mauthausen after liberation.

Meanwhile, the Americans gave us some bedding, blankets, anything to make our lives, for the time being, more bearable. They could not do enough for us. They too cried bitter tears for us.

I stayed in Mauthausen for two to four weeks. They brought people in from the village of Mauthausen to show them the crematoria, the barracks, the piles of dead bodies. These Austrian townspeople said they had no idea as to what was going on in the camp; they did not know that there was a camp. The crematoria were going full blast twenty-four hours a day, and one could see the smoke miles away—but they didn't see anything, they didn't know anything.

Moving Again

There were rumors that the Russians were coming to this part of Austria. A Dr. Lipshitz, an Army doctor, told us to get out as soon as possible. He said that we could go by American military bus to Linz. He took as many of us as possible to the American zone. I met my brothers in Linz.

I arrived in the United States, in November 1949, on the Navy ship Marine Jumper. On the high seas I thought I was going to die. I was so sick. Through five concentration camps I always had hope—it was on my way to a new life that I thought I was not going to make it. But I did!

A survivor and a U.S. Army doctor in the women's camp at Mauthausen, Austria, May 1945.

chapter five

Paul Parks

Paul Parks was born in Indianapolis, Indiana. Paul has two sisters, Jacquelyn and Dorothy Jean.

Paul's father, a Seminole Indian, was an Army scout during World War I. After the war he returned to his reservation in Florida. Paul's mother was part Creek Indian and part black. His parents moved to Indiana because of the promise of work. Soon after their arrival, Paul's father came down with tuberculosis.

Paul's mother completed community college in Marion, Indiana. After nursing Paul's father back to health, his mother got a job in the Work Projects Administration (WPA) program. She became involved in the anti-lynching movement in the South.

My father never acculturated to life outside of the reservation. He wanted to fish and hunt, and he believed his children should do the same. My mother insisted that education and knowledge would bring us success in Western, European-based American society.

My mother constantly walked my two sisters and me to the library. I even won a prize for having read the most books in a summer. My mother just kept on buying me books on how to become: on American business, on American people, geography, and history. We were very poor. Let me say it this way: we didn't have any money, but we had a strong cultural base.

We learned all the traditional Indian customs in the house, although, on the streets, we were looked at as black by the whites and as outsiders by the blacks.

We lived in a totally black neighborhood. Teachers, fire chiefs, and policemen were all black. There were only two white families: Daniel's—he became a very dear friend—and the grocer's family, the Segals, Orthodox Jews. Gabe Segal allowed my family to run a tab when funds were limited and, as I grew up, he gave me a job plucking chickens.

Since we lived in an all-black neighborhood, the first discrimination I encountered was from the black community. Daniel and I would stand, back to back, and fight off the neighborhood kids. The kids would bait me because of my Indian background, and I would never walk away. I was tough. I had to be to survive, to protect myself and my family.

Finally, a math teacher in high school, Grant Parker, took me under his wing. He encouraged me. I had good math skills, so he enrolled me in every kind of math class. Mr. Parker took me home with him to work for his family, so that I would have some pocket money for clothes.

I joined the debate team, and I became a good debater, but my team wasn't allowed to win the championship, although everyone said that we were the best. The white judges just wouldn't give it to us. Mr. Parker helped me get a scholarship to Purdue University. I also won scholarships for my oratorial skills and from a Veteran's Association.

Three hundred and twenty-two of us graduated from high school, and all but twelve of us finished college.

Determination

I didn't have the money for the train fare and the room and board for college. Mr. Segal paid for it and sent me money once a month. When I finally got to Purdue, the campus was segregated: living assignments, discussion groups, and strong rules about going out with white women.

I was in the bookstore my freshman year, 1941, and the beauty queen came up to me, putting her arms around my neck to welcome me. I froze. I saw myself being kicked out of school for being seen with a white girl. No one ever said anything about it, but I spent every day for a week waiting to see a suspension letter in my mailbox.

I got four or five hours' sleep a night. I studied very hard, but the university administration did not want me to become an engineer. There were no jobs for black engineers, they said. Although I should have been deferred from the draft in 1942 because I was in college, my dean would not exempt me. I had been causing trouble on campus, petitioning for the rights of blacks to be housed in the dormitories. The dean thought the Army was a good way to get rid of me.

I stormed into his office, angry that the sealed letter he gave me was not the exemption I had expected, and screamed, "I'll be back!" The dean said, "That's not necessarily so, because not everybody that goes to war comes back." I think the drive I had all through the Army was due to my determination to graduate from that school.

Discrimination at Home and Abroad

I had been trained in Virginia, in the Quartermaster Corps, as a motor machinist. I was sent overseas instead of to officer training school or back to college after basic training. I had gotten into trouble defending a black lady on a bus and created a riot.

Life in the Army in the South was completely segregated for the black soldiers. Even on the trains we were put up front so that the soot from the coal engines would dirty our faces. We had to pull the shades down over the windows so that white folk wouldn't try and take shots at us from the train stations. Drinking fountains and bathrooms were segregated. Eventually I was shipped over to Scotland and placed with the 365th Engineers.

When I got to Weybridge, in Cornwall, England, I experienced one of the nicest times I had had up to that point in my life. I met the bishop of a Methodist Church, Reverend Harvey, and I became a part of his family. I devoured the books in his library. He brought me on tours around the countryside, he made me a birthday party, and

I remember one incident, in particular, when I was on patrol with four men from my Army unit, and we were suddenly surrounded by German soldiers. At first I thought that we might as well give up. Somehow Purdue came into my mind, and I remember telling the four men I was with to take the reeds off the bank of the river and put them in their mouths so we could slip under the water and breathe. We stayed there while the twenty Germans on patrol crossed the bridge. I had learned about the reeds from my father. Luckily, we got back to camp undetected.

constantly wrote my mother about me. In the Army, I learned to excavate mines and booby traps. I was there about a year, and my unit ended up in the same camp as the 82nd Airborne.

My unit was out one evening at a party in town. As we were leaving, a jeep from the 82nd came by with a machine gun mounted on it. A soldier in it fired at a young white British lady coming out of the dance with a black soldier. They were killed. Every night fighting broke out within the Army. People were beat up and killed, both black and white folk. The Army took measures to separate the troops. The black men were sent downtown, and the white men were sent to the suburbs. The separation continued until they told us to pack up because we were going to be part of an invasion—Normandy.

The Normandy Invasion

Just after midnight on June 6, 1944, British and American airborne forces flew to German-occupied northern France. They landed behind the German forces along the coast. After daybreak, they were followed by seaborne American and British troops.

While Allied naval guns and bombers attacked the German beach defenses, Allied soldiers swarmed ashore. The operation was enormous: 4,000 transports, 800 warships, countless small craft, and more than 11,000 aircraft were involved. Thousands of troops were killed. But the Allies were successful.

The Normandy Invasion gave the Allied forces a foothold in western Europe. Now Germany had to fight the Americans and British in the west as well as the Russians in the east. Paul was part of the Normandy Invasion.

We landed in Normandy on D-Day, June 6, 1944. Days later I took part in the liberation of Paris and a few months later I fought in the Battle of the Bulge at Aachen, Germany, near Belgium. We opened the roads, taking out German mines, so that the tanks could go into battle. We built bridges and blew up buildings and power plants. It was all about taking land.

We were on the front lines. We lost a lot of men. We were six companies. All the enlisted men were black, and the officers were white. I was a platoon sergeant at this point, in charge of 120 men in a First Army infantry division.

A journalist from Stars and Stripes *once asked me, "How do you keep on doing all this, with the discrimination and all?" I told him that I was eighteen years old and committed to doing the best job I could because I wanted to have the right to fight for my rights when I got back home.*

I have always been determined to fight discrimination, but I have never become bitter. My mother taught me that being bitter would waste my life and my ability to think and react—to do the things that are necessary to survive in this society.

American troops land on the beaches of Normandy, France, June 6, 1944.

An Accidental Visit

In April 1945, my commander told me to go down to the company engineering team outside of Munich. I was an expert on German metallic mines, and they wanted me to teach a team of men how to deactivate the mines.

While I was in Munich, we got an order to go and take a camp. They loaded up the trucks and asked me to go with them. It was an accident that I went to Dachau. We thought it would be a military camp. We were totally unprepared.

On April 29, 1945, we drove up the road of the camp, seeing no one. We heard gunfire coming from the other side of the camp. Apparently, there were some German guards still fighting with our troops. As we drove forward, people started coming out of the barracks clothed in striped suits. At first, we thought that they were German criminals. They tried to hug us, and we pushed them away. They were so filthy.

Finally, a person spoke in English to me, a rabbi. He told me that he was so happy that we were here because now he knew he wasn't going to die. I noticed the dead bodies stacked up against the walls, and he began to tell me the story of the concentration camp. We sat down together along the road, and he told me all about it. My mind was going back to the Battle of the Bulge and how the Germans had overrun American hospitals, killed all the doctors and nurses, and just left them there.

Then I started to liken his story to American slavery. I told him that for 300 years ancestors of mine could not make a decision about when to get up or go to bed. They worked when they were told to do so, and when somebody killed them, the murderer knew that he or she had complete control over the slave's life.

The most barbaric thing I saw was a row of little conical-shaped things inside some storage room. When I got closer, I realized that it was people's gold teeth. For me, that was the end—the most revolting issue demonstrating people's barbarism.

Background photo: Boxes of gold crowns and dentures removed from the bodies of prisoners in Buchenwald concentration camp.

Survivors of the Dachau concentration camp sit on the steps of a barrack after liberation.

Grim Work

Soon I was put to work. Our soldiers were told to dig trenches and, with bulldozers, get the bodies, after identification, into these ditches. We buried them all. I was there a few weeks. We were the engineers, and this became our job. We stayed in Dachau all day and returned at night to sleep at an Army field station near the camp.

I talked a lot with the rabbi. He talked about the horrible things that were done to the people. Our conversations made me think about the German soldiers that we had captured along the way. They were intelligent and well educated. Some spoke three languages. They asked for classical music records, and cried as they listened. It made me wonder about man's relationship to man. How, morally, could they have done what they did?

A cart laden with human corpses from Dachau concentration camp is driven through the nearby town of Dachau. Allied officers required local farmers to transport the bodies of the deceased through the town to the burial site.

chapter six

Everyone who was an eyewitness to the horrors that were perpetrated on innocent people by the Nazis was deeply affected. Most people find it difficult to talk about the scenes they witnessed. They had to distance themselves from this terrible time in our history in order to move forward and lead productive lives.

Irving Roth and his parents came to the United States in January 1947. He became an engineer. Today, he says, "It was not until much later, many years later, that I gradually developed an understanding, philosophically, about what had happened. The hatred that surrounded me and the inability of anyone to come to my aid during the war wasn't truly digested by me until I began to talk about my personal experiences."

Irving recently retired from the UNISYS Corporation. Today, he is director of education at the Holocaust Memorial and Educational Center of Nassau County. He, his wife, children, and grandchildren are grateful for his ability to enjoy and treasure every day of his survival since his liberation from Buchenwald in 1945.

Jim Van Raalte is retired from the Van Raalte Company. He is a deacon at his church and enjoys his life with his wife, sons, and grandchildren. He realizes the importance of recounting the experiences he had as a soldier during World War II. Jim wants

Nina Krieger

Halina Bryks

Moszek Sztajnkeier

Angela Gogolin

Beno Traub

Szlama Kleinman

Survivors began to rebuild their lives after recovering physically from the devastation of the Holocaust. These teens in the Children's Center No. 182 at Indersdorf, Germany, display their names in hope that a surviving relative will recognize them.

American students to know that prejudice and hate lead to killing and war. "For over forty years, I didn't say a thing about walking into a concentration camp. I guess I was suppressing the memories of my experience. I didn't want to think about it."

Jim started discussing what had happened after he was approached by the Holocaust Education Center in Glen Cove, New York. "They asked if I had any artifacts from the time I had been involved with the liberation of Buchenwald. I gave them the Nazi flag I had taken from the camp, with the signatures of all the guys in my squad on it. I handed over a transcribed copy of one of the letters I had written home and a few photographs from that time. It was a cathartic experience to talk about it all and finally relate some of it to my sons. They couldn't believe what I had been through."

Helen Tilles' three brothers and one sister, Sophie, also survived the war. However, most of their families were murdered by the Nazis.

Helen and Albert were reunited during the liberation of Mauthausen. There Dr. Albert Tilles assisted the American doctors. He and Helen had married quickly during the war and had been forced apart by circumstance. They now resumed their life together and moved to the United States. They have one son and three grandchildren.

Helen, who survived the camps, in part because of her secretarial and language skills, has a message for all of us: "Study, learn—knowledge can't be taken away from you. Don't think only about yourself, but how what you do affects others. Live with hope!"

After Paul Parks returned from the war, he finished his degree in engineering at Purdue and then earned a master's degree and doctorate. He became active in the civil rights movement, working closely with Martin Luther King Jr. He has continued to speak out about the Holocaust. "I really wanted to spread the word about the Holocaust. You cannot let bigotry continue. My father always said, 'Don't blame a person for something they cannot do anything about. If you are bigoted, you are ignorant!'"

Paul now lives in Massachusetts and is active in his engineering consulting firm. He is proud of the accomplishments of his children.

Each person who was liberated from a Nazi concentration camp

Gabriel Padawer poses beside his bar mitzvah gifts in Munich, Germany, 1937. Gabriel's family left Germany for the United States in 1938. Six years later, in 1944, Gabriel returned to Germany as an American GI.

or who liberated someone else recognizes in a deep and unique way the value of freedom.

As Jim observes, "It is very important that future generations understand the importance of these events and learn enough about them. They need the tools, the knowledge we can share with them, to prevent these terrible moments in our history from reoccurring."

Timeline

January 30, 1933	Adolf Hitler is appointed chancellor of Germany.
March 23, 1933	Dachau, the first concentration camp, is built to hold political opponents of Nazis.
April 1, 1933	Nazis proclaim a daylong boycott of Jewish-owned businesses.
July 14, 1933	Nazis outlaw all other political parties in Germany; a law is passed legalizing forced sterilization of Roma and Sinti (Gypsies), mentally and physically disabled Germans, African-Germans, and others.
January 26, 1934	Germany and Poland sign Non-Aggression Pact.
August 1, 1935	"No Jews" signs appear in Germany forbidding Jews from stores, restaurants, places of entertainment, etc.
September 15, 1935	German parliament passes the Nuremberg Laws.
March 13, 1938	Germany annexes Austria.
September 29, 1938	Munich Conference: Britain and France allow Hitler to annex part of Czechoslovakia in order to prevent war.
November 9, 1938	Kristallnacht (looting and vandalism of Jewish homes and businesses and wholesale destruction of synagogues) occurs throughout Germany and Austria; 30,000 Jews are sent to Nazi concentration camps.
March 15, 1939	Germany invades all of Czechoslovakia.
August 23, 1939	Germany and Soviet Union sign Non-Aggression Pact.
September 1, 1939	Germany invades western Poland.
September 2, 1939	Great Britain and France declare war on Germany.
September 17, 1939	Soviet Union invades eastern Poland.

Spring 1940	Germany invades Denmark, Norway, Holland, Luxembourg, Belgium, and France.
March 24, 1941	Germany invades North Africa.
April 6, 1941	Germany invades Yugoslavia and Greece.
June 22, 1941	Germany invades western Soviet Union.
July 31, 1941	Reinhard Heydrich appointed to carry out the "Final Solution" (extermination of all European Jews).
Summer 1941	Einsatzgruppen (mobile killing squads) begin to massacre Jews in western Soviet Union.
December 7, 1941	Japan bombs Pearl Harbor; United States enters World War II.
January 20, 1942	Wannsee Conference: Nazi leaders meet to design "Final Solution."
Spring and Summer 1942	
	Many Polish ghettos emptied; residents deported to death camps.
February 2, 1943	German troops in Stalingrad, Soviet Union, surrender; the Allies begin to win the war.
June 11, 1943	Nazis decide that all ghettos in Poland and Soviet Union are to be emptied and residents deported to death camps.
March 19, 1944	Germany occupies Hungary.
June 6, 1944	D-Day: Normandy Invasion by the Allies.
May 8, 1945	Germany surrenders to the Allies; war ends in Europe.

Glossary

Allied troops British, French, Soviet, and U.S. armies united in Europe to fight Nazi Germany during World War II.

Appel *See Zeilappell.*

Appelplatz Area in a concentration camp where inmates were lined up for attendance taking.

block Barrack in a concentration camp or death camp

Blockälteste Prisoner in charge of a barrack in a concentration camp or death camp.

Buchenwald concentration camp Located outside of Weimar, Germany, Buchenwald was opened by the Nazis on July 17, 1937, and liberated by American troops on April 11, 1945.

burial pits Mass graves.

camps In the Nazi system of imprisonment, there were labor, concentration, transit, and death camps; people were placed in these camps against their will because of prejudice, and they were treated inhumanely.

commissary Store where food, clothing, or supplies are kept in a camp.

crematorium (plural: crematoria) Oven in Nazi concentration camps and death camps used to burn the corpses of inmates.

Dachau concentration camp Located near the town of Dachau, Germany, it was opened by the Nazis on March 22, 1933, and liberated by American troops on April 29, 1945.

D-Day Day on which a military operation is to take place; in World War II, the day of the invasion of Normandy, France, June 6, 1944.

death march Forced march undertaken by camp inmates as the Germans tried to outrun the advancing Allied armies; most inmates did not survive the marches.

dysentery Intestinal disease characterized by stomach pain and diarrhea.

gas chamber Large locked room designed to murder people on a mass scale by the use of poison gas Zyklon B.

infantry Branch of army with soldiers trained to fight on foot.

Kleinelager "Little camp"; the block for younger people at Buchenwald concentration camp.

noncom Noncommissioned officer; subordinate officer (such as sergeant) in the army, air force, or marine corps who is appointed from among the enlisted men or women.

panzer division German armored division of World War II that featured German panzer tanks.

Signal Corps Branch of Army concerned with communications.

Stars and Stripes American army magazine published for the soldiers.

Weimar City in Germany where a democratic German government was established after World War I; Buchenwald was located nearby.

Zeilappell Often cruel roll call of inmates in concentration camps.

For Further Reading

Altschuler, David A. *Hitler's War Against the Jews*. West Orange, NJ: Behrman House, 1978.

Drucker, Malka, and Michael Halperin. *Jacob's Rescue: A Holocaust Story*. New York: Bantam Doubleday Dell, 1993.

Eisenberg, Azriel. *The Lost Generation: Children in the Holocaust*. New York: Pilgrim Press, 1982.

Eliach, Yaffa. *Hasidic Tales of the Holocaust*. New York: Random House, 1988.

Frank, Anne. *Diary of a Young Girl: The Definitive Edition*. New York: Doubleday, 1995.

Holliday, Laurel. *Children in the Holocaust and World War II: Their Secret Diaries*. New York: Washington Square Press, 1994.

Jules, Jacqueline. *The Grey Striped Shirt: How Grandma and Grandpa Survived the Holocaust*. Los Angeles: Alef Design, 1994.

Klein, Gerda. *All but My Life*. New York: Hill & Wang, 1995.

Marks, Jane. *The Hidden Children: The Secret Survivors of the Holocaust*. New York: Ballantine Books, 1993.

Matas, Carol. *Daniel's Story*. New York: Simon and Schuster, 1996.

Rochman, Hazel, and Darlene Z. McCampbell, eds. *Bearing Witness: Stories of the Holocaust.* New York: Orchard Books Watts, 1995.

Roth-Hano, Renee. *Touch Wood.* New York: Puffin Books, 1989.

Wiesel, Elie. *Night.* New York: Bantam Books, 1982.

Wilkomirski, Benjamin. *Fragments.* New York: Schocken Books, 1996.

For Advanced Readers

Asscher-Pinkhof, Clara. *Star Children.* Detroit: Wayne State University Press, 1986.

Baumel, Judith Tydor. *Unfulfilled Promise: Rescue and Resettlement of Jewish Refugee Children in the United States, 1934–1945.* Juneau, Alaska: Denali Press 1990.

Dwork, Deborah. *Children with a Star.* New Haven, CT: Yale University Press, 1991.

Edelheit, Abraham J., and Herschel Edelheit. *History of the Holocaust: A Handbook and Dictionary.* Boulder, CO: Westview Press, 1994.

Gilbert, Martin. *The Holocaust: A History of the Jews of Europe During the Second World War.* New York: Henry Holt & Co., 1985.

I Never Saw Another Butterfly: Children's Drawings and Poems from Theresienstadt Concentration Camp. New York: McGraw-Hill, 1964.

Noakes, J., and G. Pridham. *Nazism: A History in Documents and Eyewitness Accounts, Vols. I and II.* New York: Pantheon Books, 1984.

Videos

Holocaust: Liberation of Auschwitz
The liberation of Auschwitz was filmed by the Soviets. Commentary describes the selection process, the medical experiments, daily life at Auschwitz, and impressions of the liberation. Note: Highly graphic. (Available from Zenger Videos, 10200 Jefferson Boulevard, Room 902, P. O. Box 802, Culver City, CA 90232, (800) 421-4246.)

More Than Broken Glass: Memories of Kristallnacht
Using archival footage and photographs and interviews with survivors, this video explores the persecution of Jews in Germany before and during the Holocaust. (Available from Ergo Media, Inc., P. O. Box 2037, Teaneck, NJ 07666; (800) 695-3746.)

Opening the Gates of Hell
American liberators share their memories of liberation. Interviews are combined with photos and footage showing camps liberated by Americans: Buchenwald, Dachau, Landsberg, Mauthausen, and Nordhausen. Note: Highly graphic. (Available from Ergo Media, Inc., P. O. Box 2037, Teaneck, NJ 07666; (800) 695-3746.)

Safe Haven
This video profiles America's only refugee camp for victims of Nazi terror. Nearly 1,000 refugees were brought to Oswego, NY, and incarcerated in a camp known as Fort Ontario for eighteen months. (Available from the Anti-Defamation League, 823 United Nations Plaza, New York, NY 10017; (212) 885-7700.)

Shoah
This film includes interviews with victims, perpetrators, and bystanders, and takes viewers to camps, towns, and railways that were part of the Holocaust. (Available in most video stores and many libraries.)

Web Sites

Anti-Defamation League—Braun Holocaust Institute
http://www.adl.org/Braun/braun.htm

Holocaust Education and Memorial Centre of Toronto
http://www.feduja.org

Museum of Tolerance
www.wiesenthal.com/mot/index.html

Simon Wiesenthal Center
http://www.wiesenthal.com/

United States Holocaust Memorial Museum
http://www.ushmm.org/index.html

Yad Vashem
http://www.yad-vashem.org.il

Index

About the Author

Tina Tito was born in Vienna, Austria, in 1948. Both of her parents were teenagers during the Shoah (Holocaust). Her father fled from Poland, surviving in Siberian labor camps. Her mother escaped the Lvov ghetto and survived by living beneath the dirt floor of the Ukrainian farmers who hid her.

Ms. Tito finished her college education in the United States and has lived and traveled extensively in Europe and Israel. For the last twenty-five years she has dedicated her life to informing people—through interviews, lectures, writing, and teaching—about the facts concerning the Shoah.

About the Series Editor

Yaffa Eliach is Professor of History and Literature in the Department of Judaic Studies at Brooklyn College. She founded and directed the Center for Holocaust Studies (now part of the Museum of Jewish Heritage—A Living Memorial to the Holocaust) and designed the Tower of Life exhibit at the U.S. Holocaust Memorial Museum. Professor Eliach is the author of *Hasidic Tales of the Holocaust; We Were Children Just Like You; There Once Was a World: A Nine Century Chronicle of the Shtetl of Eishyshok;* and *The Liberators: Eyewitness Accounts of the Liberation of Concentration Camps.*

Photo Credits

Cover photo courtesy of the Olga Abraham File © Yaffa Eliach Collection donated by Center for Holocaust Studies, Museum of Jewish Heritage, N.Y.; p. 6 © Archive Photos; pp. 8, 11, 12, 15, 20, 23, 29, 30–31 © National Archives, courtesy of the United States Holocaust Memorial Museum (USHMM) Photo Archives; pp. 12–13, 27 © William A. Scott III Collection, courtesy of USHMM Photo Archives; p. 14 courtesy of Irving Roth; p. 16 © Marion Koch Collection, courtesy of USHMM Photo Archives; pp. 18–19 © AP/Wide World Photos; p. 24 courtesy of Jim Van Raalte; pp. 32–33 © Main Commission for the Investigation of Nazi War Crimes, courtesy of USHMM Photo Archives; p. 33 © National Archives in Cracow, courtesy of USHMM Photo Archives; p. 34 Charlotte Chaney File, p. 51 Andre Marx Collection, p. 53 Gabriel Padawer File all © Yaffa Eliach Collection donated by Center for Holocaust Studies, Museum of Jewish Heritage, N.Y.; pp. 36, 46–47 © Arnold Bauer Barach, courtesy of USHMM Photo Archives; p. 37 © Hadassah Rosensaft Collection, courtesy of USHMM Photo Archives; p. 39 © William Corder Alston, Jr., courtesy of USHMM Photo Archives; p. 40 courtesy of Paul Parks; pp. 44–45 © Corbis-Bettmann; pp. 46–47 © Frank Manucci Collection, courtesy of USHMM; pp. 48–49 © David G. Briggs Collection, courtesy of USHMM Photo Archives.

Series Design
Kim Sonsky

Layout
Laura Murawski